M3 Mastery: The Evolution of an Icon

Etienne Psaila

M3 Mastery: The Evolution of an Icon

Cover design by Etienne Psaila

Interior layout by Etienne Psaila

Introduction to the BMW M3 Series

The Essence of the M3: A Legacy of Performance and Innovation

The BMW M3 stands as a monumental achievement in the world of automotive engineering, a symbol of the harmonious blend between everyday usability and exhilarating performance. Since its inception in the mid-1980s, the M3 has evolved from a modest, albeit spirited, racing-derived sedan to a benchmark of modern sports car design, continuously pushing the boundaries of what is expected from a performance vehicle.

The Evolution of the BMW M3

A Journey Through Time: The Evolution of an Icon

This book is a homage to the BMW M3, a car that has not just survived but thrived through multiple decades, adapting and reinventing itself while always staying true to its core ethos. From the raw and race-bred E30, through the sophisticated and powerful E46, to the turbocharged brilliance of the F80 and beyond, each generation of the M3 has brought something unique to the table, while building on the rich heritage of its predecessors.

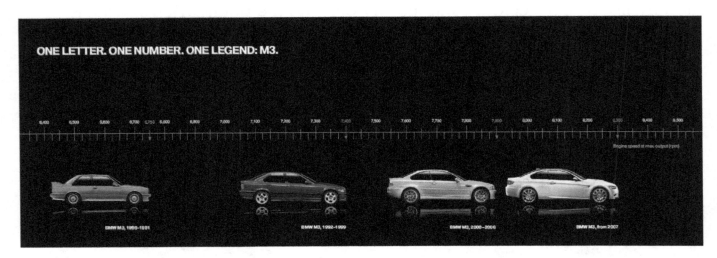

The M3 Generations

More Than Just a Car: The M3 as a Cultural Icon

Beyond its mechanical and technical accomplishments, the BMW M3 has become a cultural icon, capturing the hearts of car enthusiasts and casual admirers alike. It transcends its identity as a mere automobile to become a symbol of aspiration, performance, and technological evolution, influencing not just car culture, but also appearing in movies, video games, and as a frequent reference point in popular media.

The M3 Through the Years

A Deep Dive into the M3's Engineering and Design Philosophy

The BMW M3's story is not just about speed or power; it's about thoughtful engineering, meticulous design, and a relentless pursuit of driving pleasure. Each chapter of this book delves into the specificities of every generation, exploring the technological advancements, design philosophies, and the sheer driving joy that each M3 has offered to its enthusiasts.

E92 M3 V8 Engine

Celebrating the Community and the Future

As we look forward to the future, with anticipation for the 2024 model and beyond, this book also celebrates the vibrant community of M3 enthusiasts. From professional racers to weekend hobbyists, the M3 has garnered a diverse and passionate following, each drawn to this remarkable machine for different reasons but united by their admiration for its legacy.

BMW M3 Meets

In these pages, you will find more than just a chronicle of a car's evolution. You will discover a story of passion, innovation, and an unyielding commitment to excellence. Welcome to the world of the BMW M3, a journey through automotive history like no other.

Chapter 1: Introduction to the BMW M3

The Dawn of a Legacy

In the pantheon of automotive excellence, few names resonate as profoundly as the BMW M3. Born from the crucible of racing and refined through decades of technological innovation, the M3 is not just a car; it's a testament to the relentless pursuit of performance and luxury. Since its debut in the mid-1980s, the M3 has been a symbol of BMW's engineering prowess, blending exhilarating speed with everyday usability in a package that is as compelling to look at as it is to drive.

M3 E30 CSL

A Heritage Rooted in Racing

The story of the M3 begins with BMW's desire to dominate in touring car racing. The E30 M3 was conceived primarily as a race car, with its road-going version serving as a necessary step for homologation. This racing DNA is evident in every facet of the vehicle, from its aerodynamic bodywork to the high-revving, naturally aspirated four-cylinder engine. It set the stage for what would become a defining characteristic of all M3 generations: a seamless transition from track to road.

M3 E30 Race Car

M3 E30 at Monza

Evolution Through Generations

Each generation of the M3 has brought its own innovations while respecting the lineage that came before. From the raw power of the E30 to the refined balance of the E46 and the turbocharged prowess of the F80, the M3's journey is one of constant evolution. This chapter explores how each generation has built upon the last, not just in terms of power and performance, but in how these cars have increasingly become sophisticated, technology-laden, and luxurious, without ever losing sight of their racing roots.

M3 E30

M3 F80

The M3 in Culture and Society

Beyond the specifications and engineering feats, the M3 has embedded itself in the cultural fabric. It's a car that has been idolized in movies, video games, and by countless automotive enthusiasts across the globe. This widespread admiration goes beyond the mere performance metrics; it's about the emotional connection and the statement made by owning and driving an M3.

M3 in the Movie *Overdrive* (2017)

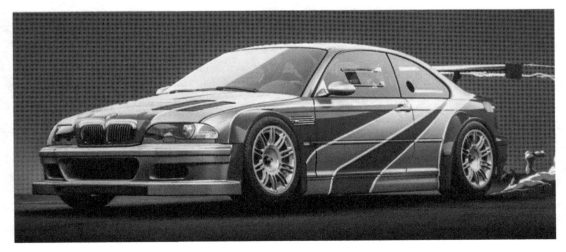

M3 in the Video Game *Need for Speed*

More Than a Car: A Symbol of Excellence

As we delve into the specifics of each M3 generation, it's important to appreciate the M3 as more than just a sum of its parts. It is a symbol of what happens when passion meets precision, when heritage meets innovation. The BMW M3 is not just a car; it's a story of ambition, a journey of continuous improvement, and a beacon for what a dedicated focus on driving pleasure can achieve.

2023 M3 CS Cockpit

In conclusion, the BMW M3 series is not just a remarkable range of high-performance cars; it is a chapter in automotive history that continues to inspire and evolve. As we turn the page to explore each generation in detail, the enduring legacy of the M3 stands as a testament to BMW's commitment to excellence.

Chapter 2: The E30 Generation (1986–1991)

The Birth of an Icon: Origins of the E30 M3

In 1986, BMW unveiled a car that would set a new standard in the world of performance vehicles: the E30 M3. Born out of the necessity for a competitive vehicle in touring car racing, the E30 M3 was a radical departure from the standard 3 Series of the time. Its journey from racetrack to road not only marked the birth of an icon but also set the tone for what would become one of the most revered lineages in automotive history.

BMW M3 E30 DTM Race Car

Racing Pedigree and Performance

The heart of the E30 M3 was its engine, a 2.3-liter inline-four that was, at its time, a marvel of engineering. This powerplant was capable of producing up to 192 horsepower, a remarkable figure for its era and size. But the M3 was more than just about power; it was about balance, agility, and precision. Its chassis was extensively reworked to provide handling characteristics that were as close to a race car as one could get in a road-legal vehicle.

BMW M3 E30 Engine

Design: Form Meets Function

Visually, the E30 M3 set itself apart with its wider wheel arches, bigger wheels, and the distinctive rear spoiler, all of which were more than just cosmetic enhancements. These changes were functional, aimed at improving aerodynamics and cooling. Inside, the M3 offered a cockpit that blended sportiness with the comfort of a luxury sedan, a balance that would become a hallmark of the M series.

The Four Cylinder E30 3-Series vs The E30 M3

E30 M3

Legacy and Impact

During its production run from 1986 to 1991, the E30 M3 not only dominated the racing circuits but also won the hearts of car enthusiasts worldwide. It became more than a car; it was a statement, a manifestation of what BMW's M division could achieve. Its success laid the groundwork for all future M3 generations, each of which would draw inspiration from this original masterpiece.

1991 BMW E30 M3 Group A: Classic GP Assen

The E30 M3 Today: A Collector's Dream

Today, the E30 M3 has achieved an almost mythical status among car collectors and enthusiasts. Its combination of racing pedigree, classic design, and driving dynamics make it a highly sought-after piece of automotive history. For many, owning an E30 M3 is not just about owning a piece of BMW's legacy but about experiencing a raw, unfiltered driving experience that is hard to find in modern cars.

BMW M3 Collectors Garage

In conclusion, the E30 M3 was more than just the first of its name. It was a groundbreaking vehicle that redefined what a sports sedan could be. Its legacy continues to influence the design and engineering of performance vehicles and it remains a shining example of BMW's commitment to driving pleasure.

BMW E30 M3

Chapter 3: The E36 Generation (1992–1999)

A New Era of Power and Refinement

The introduction of the E36 M3 in 1992 marked a significant evolution in the M3 saga. Moving beyond its predecessor's focus on raw, track-oriented performance, the E36 M3 embraced a more refined, yet equally exhilarating approach to the sports sedan concept. This generation combined greater power with advanced technology and improved comfort, making the M3 more appealing to a broader audience without sacrificing its racing heritage.

E36 M3

Technical Innovations and Performance Upgrades

At the heart of the E36 M3 lay a new engine: a 3.0-liter inline-six that initially produced 286 horsepower, later upgraded to a 3.2-liter producing 321 horsepower in subsequent models. This power unit was not just about increased displacement; it represented a leap in engineering, featuring innovative technologies like VANOS (BMW's variable valve timing system). The result was a smoother, more responsive power delivery and improved fuel efficiency.

BMW E36 M3 Engine

Design: Balancing Sportiness with Sophistication

The E36 M3's design evolved to reflect its more sophisticated demeanor. While retaining a clear visual connection to its E30 predecessor, the E36's lines were smoother and more aerodynamic. The interior also saw significant upgrades, with higher quality materials and more advanced electronic features, reflecting a shift towards a more luxurious driving experience.

E36 M3 Interior

The E36 M3 in the Global Arena

A notable change with the E36 M3 was its introduction to the North American market. This expansion was not without modifications; the US-spec M3 featured a slightly detuned engine due to emissions regulations. However, it still offered the essence of the M3's performance and quickly became a favorite among American enthusiasts.

BMW E36 M3 Race Car at Imola Circuit

The North American BMW E36 M3

Impact and Legacy of the E36 M3

Throughout its production run, the E36 M3 was celebrated for its ability to offer a balanced blend of performance, comfort, and daily usability. It appealed to a wider audience, serving not only as a weekend track car but also as a comfortable daily driver. This broader appeal helped solidify the M3's reputation not just as a performance car, but as a versatile, well-rounded sports sedan.

BMW E36 M3 at Nordschleife

BMW E36 M3 – Not only a Track Car

In summary, the E36 M3 was a pivotal chapter in the M3 story. It transitioned the model from a niche, race-bred car into a more accessible, yet no less thrilling, sports sedan. Its blend of performance, comfort, and style left a lasting impact on the automotive world and paved the way for the future evolutions of the M3 lineage.

Chapter 4: The E46 Generation (2000–2006)

A Perfect Fusion of Power and Poise

With the turn of the millennium, BMW introduced the E46 M3, a vehicle that many enthusiasts consider the zenith of the M3 lineage. Launched in 2000, the E46 M3 was a masterful blend of power, sophistication, and driving dynamics. It built upon the strengths of its predecessors while introducing a range of technological and design enhancements that elevated the M3 experience to new heights.

BMW E46 M3

Revolutionary Engineering: The Heart of the E46

The centerpiece of the E46 M3 was its 3.2-liter naturally aspirated inline-six engine, producing 343 horsepower. This engine was renowned for its high-revving character, going up to an 8,000 RPM redline, and delivering a linear power curve that was both exhilarating and accessible. Coupled with a six-speed manual transmission or the innovative SMG (Sequential M Sport Gearbox), the E46 M3 offered a driving experience that was both engaging and refined.

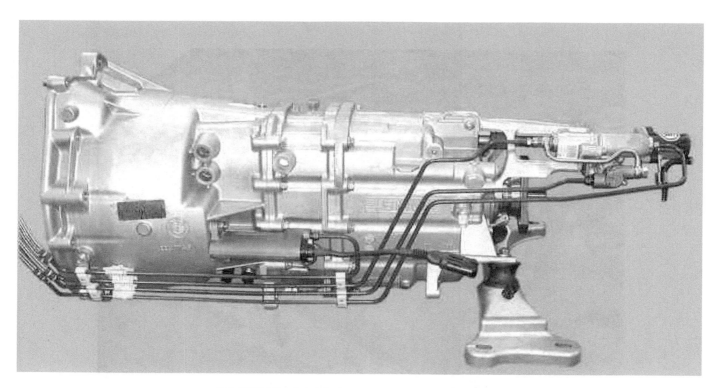

BMW E46 M3 SMG 2 Transmision

BMW E46 M3 Drivetrain

BMW E46 M3 Engine

Design Evolution: Aesthetics Meets Aerodynamics

The E46 M3 carried forward the muscular and athletic aesthetics that had become a hallmark of the M3 series. Subtle yet significant design tweaks included more pronounced wheel arches, a power dome on the hood, and the iconic quad exhaust setup. These design elements were not just for show; they enhanced the car's aerodynamic efficiency and cooling performance, making the E46 as functional as it was visually striking.

Redefining the Sports Sedan: Comfort and Performance

Inside, the E46 M3 balanced its race-inspired roots with luxury. The interior featured high-quality materials, supportive sport seats, and advanced technology for the time, including a sophisticated navigation system and a Harman Kardon sound system. This made the E46 M3 a car that could be enjoyed both on spirited weekend drives and in everyday commuting.

BMW E46 M3 Interior

The E46 M3: A Modern Classic

During its production run, the E46 M3 not only solidified its position as a benchmark in the sports car segment but also started to gain recognition as a modern classic. Its balanced approach to performance and usability, along with its naturally aspirated engine and manual transmission options, have made it a highly sought-after model among enthusiasts and collectors.

BMW E46 M3 Track Car

The E46 M3 represents a pinnacle in the M3 series, a perfect harmony of performance, design, and emotion. It stands as a testament to BMW's engineering prowess and a symbol of what makes the M3 more than just a car, but a legend in the automotive world.

Colorado Road Trip in a BMW E46 M3

Chapter 5: The E90/E92/E93 Generation (2007–2013)

The V8 Era: A Bold Step Forward

The E90/E92/E93 generation of the BMW M3, introduced between 2007 and 2013, marked a significant shift in the M3's history. For the first time, the M3 was powered by a V8 engine, departing from the traditional inline-six. This change represented BMW's commitment to pushing the boundaries of performance, while also adapting to the evolving expectations of a modern sports car.

BMW E92 M3

BMW E90 M3

BMW E93 M3

A Powerhouse Engine: The 4.0-Liter V8

The heart of this generation was its 4.0-liter V8 engine, delivering a breathtaking 420 horsepower. This engine was a marvel of engineering, featuring a high-revving design that could reach 8,400 RPM, providing an exhilarating driving experience. The sound of the V8 was equally impressive, producing a throaty roar that was music to the ears of automotive enthusiasts.

The V8 Engine in the E90/92/93

Design Evolution: Embracing Aggression and Elegance

The E90/E92/E93 generation saw the M3 available in three body styles: sedan (E90), coupe (E92), and convertible (E93). Each variant embodied a unique blend of aggression and elegance. The design featured wider fenders, a more pronounced front bumper with larger air intakes, and the iconic quad exhaust pipes. These elements not only enhanced the car's visual appeal but also improved its aerodynamic efficiency and cooling.

BMW E92 M3

Interior Sophistication Meets Sporty Ergonomics

Inside, the E90/E92/E93 M3 balanced luxury and sportiness. The interior was outfitted with high-quality materials, including leather and carbon-fiber trim options. The driver-focused cockpit was designed for both comfort and performance, featuring ergonomically designed seats and controls, ensuring that the driver remained connected to the car and the road.

BMW E92 M3 Interior

Technological Advancements: Enhancing the Driving Experience

This generation of the M3 also saw significant technological advancements. It introduced features like the M Drive system, which allowed drivers to customize settings for engine response, steering, and suspension. The optional Electronic Damping Control (EDC) provided an adaptable driving experience, suitable for both track days and daily driving.

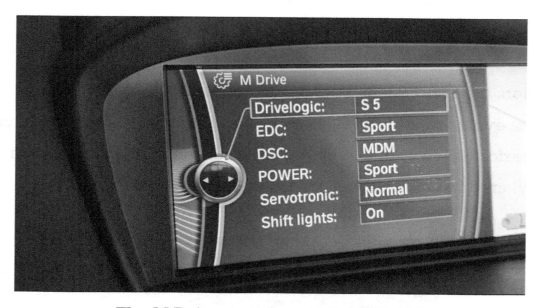

The M Drive Interface in the E92 M3

A Modern Icon: The Legacy of the E90/E92/E93 M3

The E90/E92/E93 M3 was more than just a powerful car; it was a symbol of BMW's ability to innovate and adapt. Its combination of a high-performance V8 engine, striking design, and advanced technology solidified its position as a modern icon in the automotive world. Today, it is revered by enthusiasts for its unique character and the visceral driving experience it offers.

BMW E92 M3 Track Build

In conclusion, the E90/E92/E93 generation of the BMW M3 was a bold statement of evolution and excellence. It successfully fused the raw excitement of a high-performance engine with the sophistication of modern design and technology, creating an unforgettable chapter in the M3 legacy.

2008 BMW E93 M3

Chapter 6: The F80 Generation (2014–2018)

Embracing Turbocharging: A New Chapter in Performance

The F80 M3, introduced in 2014, marked a significant turning point in the M3 lineage. BMW made a bold move by replacing the naturally aspirated engines of previous generations with a turbocharged powerplant. This transition reflected a broader trend in the automotive industry towards smaller, more efficient engines that still delivered high performance. The F80 M3 showcased BMW's ability to adapt to changing times without compromising the car's essence.

BMW F80 M3

The Turbocharged Powerhouse: 3.0-Liter Inline-Six

The heart of the F80 M3 was a 3.0-liter twin-turbocharged inline-six engine, capable of producing 425 horsepower. This engine was not only more powerful but also more efficient than the V8 it replaced. The turbochargers provided a significant increase in torque, available across a wide range of RPMs, making the F80 M3 incredibly responsive and versatile in various driving conditions.

BMW F80 M3 Engine

A Leap Forward in Design and Aerodynamics

In terms of design, the F80 M3 took an evolutionary step forward. It featured more aggressive styling cues, including a power bulge on the hood, wider fenders, and larger air intakes for improved cooling and aerodynamic efficiency. The car's stance was both menacing and elegant, a visual representation of its performance capabilities.

The BMW F80 M3 Aerodynamics

Interior: Blending Luxury with a Racing Spirit

The interior of the F80 M3 struck a fine balance between luxury and performance. It featured high-quality materials, a driver-centric layout, and advanced technology, including a new infotainment system and digital displays. The M-specific seats provided excellent support during spirited driving while ensuring comfort during longer journeys.

BMW F80 M3 Interior and Driver controls

Technological Innovations: Enhancing the M3 Experience

The F80 M3 was loaded with technological advancements that enhanced its driving dynamics. Features like the Active M Differential and Adaptive M Suspension allowed for a customizable driving experience, adaptable to both track and street settings. The introduction of these systems demonstrated BMW's commitment to combining performance with advanced technology.

Different Modes for Different Suspension and Differential Settings

The F80s Adaptability to Race Track and the Road

A New Era of M3: Performance for the Modern Age

The F80 M3 was a testament to BMW's ability to evolve and adapt while maintaining the core values of the M3 series. Its combination of turbocharged power, sophisticated design, and cutting-edge technology not only met the demands of the modern driver but also set a new standard for what a performance sedan could be.

F80 M3 on Track

F80 M3 in the City

In conclusion, the F80 M3 represented a significant evolution in the M3 story. It successfully embraced the challenges of modern automotive engineering, delivering a vehicle that was powerful, efficient, and technologically advanced, while still capturing the spirit and excitement that has always defined the M3.

Chapter 7: The G80 Generation (2021–Present)

The M3 Reimagined: A Bold Leap into the Future

The launch of the G80 M3 in 2021 marked a new era for BMW's iconic sports sedan. Embracing a radical design and engineering approach, the G80 M3 set out to redefine what a modern performance car could be. It combined BMW's rich heritage with cutting-edge technology, resulting in a vehicle that was both a departure from and a homage to its illustrious predecessors.

BMW G80 M3

Performance Redefined: The Return of the Inline-Six

At the core of the G80 M3 was a return to the inline-six configuration, this time with a 3.0-liter twin-turbocharged engine. Available in two states of tune – the standard 473 horsepower and the Competition model's 503 horsepower – this engine offered a blend of explosive power and refined delivery. Coupled with advanced drivetrain technology, including the option of all-wheel drive for the first time, the G80 M3 delivered performance that was both exhilarating and accessible.

BMW G80 M3 Engine

A Design Revolution: Embracing Controversy and Character

The G80 M3 introduced one of the most significant design overhauls in the model's history. The most notable change was the oversized kidney grille, a bold statement that sparked much discussion among enthusiasts and critics alike. This striking design was complemented by a muscular body, aerodynamic enhancements, and distinctive lines, all of which contributed to a look that was unmistakably M3.

BMW G80 M3's Controversial Grille

The G80 M3 Muscular Body

Luxury Meets High-Tech: The G80's Cabin

The interior of the G80 M3 was a masterpiece of luxury and technology. It featured premium materials, highly adjustable sport seats, and a state-of-the-art infotainment system. The driver-focused cockpit was designed to enhance the driving experience, blending intuitive controls with advanced digital displays.

BMW G80 M3 Interior

Technological Mastery: Driving Dynamics for the Modern Age

The G80 M3 showcased BMW's latest advancements in automotive technology. From its sophisticated suspension system to the M xDrive all-wheel-drive system available in the Competition model, these technologies provided unparalleled driving dynamics. They offered drivers the ability to tailor their driving experience to their preferences, whether on the road or the track.

The M xDrive System

The G80's Settings Interface

Setting New Standards: The G80 M3's Place in History

The G80 M3 was more than just a new chapter in the M3 story; it was a statement of BMW's vision for the future of performance cars. Balancing tradition with innovation, the G80 M3 set new standards in terms of performance, design, and technology, continuing the M3's legacy as a benchmark in the automotive world.

The G80 as a Track Day Car

In conclusion, the G80 M3 represented a bold step forward for the M3 series. It challenged conventions and set new benchmarks, all while maintaining the essence of what has always made the M3 special: a commitment to driving excellence. As a blend of BMW's racing DNA and a vision for the future, the G80 M3 stands as a testament to the enduring legacy of the M3 series.

BMW G80 M3 on the Road

Chapter 8: The Future - The 2024 Model and Beyond

Anticipating the Next Evolution

As we look towards the future, the BMW M3 continues to stand at the forefront of automotive evolution. The upcoming 2024 model is eagerly anticipated, promising to push the boundaries of what we've come to expect from this iconic series. While specifics are still shrouded in the anticipation of its unveiling, the 2024 M3 is poised to embrace the latest in automotive technology and design, continuing the M3's legacy of setting industry standards.

2024 BMW M3 CS

Innovation in the Age of Electrification

The future of the M3 is inevitably intertwined with the broader automotive industry's shift towards electrification. BMW has already demonstrated its commitment to electric vehicles with models like the i4 and iX. It's plausible to expect that the 2024 M3 and subsequent models will incorporate some form of electric propulsion, whether in the form of hybrid technology or a fully electric powertrain, blending traditional M3 performance with modern environmental consciousness.

The BMW i7 M70 xDrive Electric Sedan with 660hp revealed in 2023

The First Electric BMW M3 confirmed for 2027 and is expected to ride on BMW's next-gen Neue Klasse Platform

BMW CEO Oliver Zipse next to Vision Neue Klasse concept

Design Philosophies: The Future Aesthetic

The design of future M3 models will continue to reflect BMW's evolving design language. Building on the bold steps taken with the G80, the 2024 M3 is expected to feature even more refined aerodynamics, advanced materials, and a design that balances aggression with elegance. The exterior will likely be a statement piece, indicative of BMW's vision for the future of performance vehicles.

2024 BMW M3 CS

Technological Advancements: Driving into the Future

Technological innovation will be at the heart of the 2024 M3. This could include advancements in autonomous driving features, connectivity, and interactive interfaces. The integration of these technologies will aim to enhance the driving experience, ensuring that the M3 remains at the cutting edge of both performance and convenience.

2024 BMW M3 Controls

Epilogue: The Enduring Legacy of the BMW M3

A Journey Through Excellence

As we reach the conclusion of this exploration into the BMW M3 series, it's clear that the M3 is more than just a series of cars. It's a journey through the evolution of automotive excellence, a reflection of BMW's unrelenting pursuit of perfection. From the raw, race-bred E30 to the sophisticated and technologically advanced G80, each generation of the M3 has left an indelible mark on the automotive world.

The M3: From First to Sixth Generation

The M3: More Than a Car, a Cultural Icon

The M3 has transcended its status as a mere automobile to become a cultural icon. It has influenced not just the world of car enthusiasts but also the wider realms of media, fashion, and lifestyle. The M3's journey mirrors the changing times and tastes, yet it consistently remains a symbol of performance, innovation, and a certain intangible allure that captivates people from all walks of life.

2011 BMW E93 M3 in the Movie *Abduction* (2011)

BMW F80 M3 in *Mission Impossible: Rogue Nation* (2015)

Embracing the Future

As BMW continues to innovate and lead in the automotive industry, the future of the M3 is undoubtedly filled with excitement and promise. The series will continue to evolve, embracing new technologies and design philosophies, yet the core essence of the M3 – the pursuit of ultimate driving pleasure – will remain unchanged. The M3 will continue to set benchmarks, challenge conventions, and inspire generations of drivers and enthusiasts.

BMW iM3 Concept

Electric M3 Concept

A Testament to BMW's Legacy

The story of the M3 is a testament to BMW's engineering prowess, design philosophy, and understanding of what drivers desire. It is a narrative of how a car can evolve over decades, not just in response to changing technologies and regulations but also in how it can continue to stir the souls of those who drive it.

BMW Headquarters in Munich

BMW Assembly Lines

The End of a Chapter, Not the Story

As this book closes, it's important to remember that the story of the M3 is far from over. The M3 will continue to evolve, surprise, and delight. It will continue to be more than just a car; it will be a story, a legend, and a constant reminder of what is possible when passion meets innovation.

In conclusion, the BMW M3 series represents the epitome of automotive passion and engineering excellence. Its journey through the past, present, and into the future is not just the story of a car but a narrative of ambition, innovation, and the joy of driving. As we turn the final page, we look forward with anticipation to the next chapter in the illustrious saga of the BMW M3.

Appendix: From the E30 to the G80

E30 M3

E36 M3

E46 M3

E90 M3

E92 M3

E93 M3

F80 M3

G80 M3

About the Author

Etienne Psaila, an accomplished author with over two decades of experience, has mastered the art of weaving words across various genres. His journey in the literary world has been marked by a diverse array of publications, demonstrating not only his versatility but also his deep understanding of different thematic landscapes. However, it's in the realm of automotive literature that Etienne truly combines his passions, seamlessly blending his enthusiasm for cars with his innate storytelling abilities.

Specializing in automotive books, Etienne brings to life the world of automobiles through his eloquent prose and an array of stunning, high-quality color photographs. His works are a tribute to the automotive industry, capturing its evolution, technological advancements, and the sheer beauty of vehicles in a manner that is both informative and visually captivating.

A proud alumnus of the University of Malta, Etienne's academic background lays a solid foundation for his meticulous research and factual accuracy. His education has not only enriched his writing but has also fueled his career as a dedicated teacher. In the classroom, just as in his writing, Etienne strives to inspire, inform, and ignite a passion for learning.

As a teacher, Etienne harnesses his experience in writing to engage and educate, bringing the same level of dedication and excellence to his students as he does to his readers. His dual role as an educator and author makes him uniquely positioned to understand and convey complex concepts with clarity and ease, whether in the classroom or through the pages of his books.

Through his literary works, Etienne Psaila continues to leave an indelible mark on the world of automotive literature, captivating car enthusiasts and readers alike with his insightful perspectives and compelling narratives.

Made in the USA
Monee, IL
23 May 2024

58832004R00044